GODDESS LAND:
The First Ten Years

PublishAmerica
Baltimore

© 2006 Athena Angelic.
All rights reserved. No part of this book may be reproduced, stored in a retrieval system or transmitted in any form or by any means without the prior written permission of the publishers, except by a reviewer who may quote brief passages in a review to be printed in a newspaper, magazine or journal.

First printing

At the specific preference of the author, PublishAmerica allowed this work to remain exactly as the author intended, verbatim, without editorial input.

ISBN: 1-4137-9886-1
PUBLISHED BY PUBLISHAMERICA, LLLP
www.publishamerica.com
Baltimore

Printed in the United States of America

Dedicated to Kristina Heinz

Thank you for all the love,
understanding, and encouragement
a daughter could ever ask for.

I would be lost without you.

Contents

Chapter 1: *Random Thoughts* 5
    The Incidentals of Life

Chapter 2: *Divine Guidance* 51
    Inspiration for the Eradicated Soul

Chapter 3: *Love Worth Finding* 75
    Remembering the Reasons We Love to Love

Chapter 4: *Opposites Attract* 119
    Remembering the Reasons We Hate to Love

Chapter 5: *Desert Desolation* 145
    Feeling the Pains of Everyday Life

Chapter 6: *My Animosity Amuses Me* 179
    Hate, Revenge, and Wrath

Chapter 1:

Random Thoughts

Hearts cannot be trusted,
for human hearts will fail.
Only time will tell,
if truth will prevail.

Immortality

I'm hungry now, I have a need
Let me out, so I can feed
Blood will drip so slowly down
I will smile, you will frown.
I'm sorry that you cannot live
But this gift, I cannot give.
Immortality is really quite rare.
Plus, for you, I do not care.
You are nothing more than food
I'm sorry if I'm being rude.
My sly smile will never give me away
You best get running, do not stay.
For if you do, you will be mine.
On your flesh, I will dine.
Give me life and give me strength
You pitiful humans are out-ranked.
Let the lights burn slowly out
Run and beg and scream and shout.
For we are atop the great food chain
We feel pleasure, you feel pain.
Look in my eyes, and you will see
Why you now belong to me.
    (1-14-2005)

Fear

Into the dark, I walk, alone and afraid.
Ugly and lurking creatures creep, at every shadow made.
Turning around, jumping in fright, I'm scared to be alone.
Alone in the dark, without a friend in the world, so far away from home.
Home is gone and so I walk, away from the crowd.
Little did I know that prowlers walk too,
But without making any sound.
I screamed and ran as I felt it, trying to reach for me.
But looking back I see a defenseless man, not an enemy.
Remember though, that things are not,
Always what they seem to be.
For my trusting heart and caring soul, brought death upon me.
That man, I thought, so helpless and out of place,
Killed me off and left my body, without leaving any trace.
They never found that man, who murdered me on the spot.
I'm now a ghost who haunts the living,
Maybe I should have fought.
I've lost my life and come to warn you, so you don't lose yours.
Be careful where you go, don't trust the dark,
it betrays the kindest of souls.
   (2-26-1996)

-1 (Negative One)

feeling Inferior to all those around
how they stare and taunt and surround
you with their Perfectness
their perfect body and gorgeous face
and wonderful life how your
Life is No Life unless it can
be like theirs you are so
jealous that it drives you numb
because you realize you'll
never be Number One.
(1-13-1998)

Do You Believe?

God…what is God exactly?
A power? A belief? An attempt at guidance?
So many different Gods and beliefs grace this Earth.
But who knows they are there?
God…the almighty, the all powerful, and all knowing;
he does everything for a reason.
What reason could hurt and pain and destruction have?

Do you believe in God?
Do you believe of a power higher than yourself?
If so…why?
Why would there be a heaven?
Why would there be a hell?
They say to repent your sins to live in heaven.
But sins are our weaknesses that we endure;
our mistakes we make.
But aren't all supposed to make mistakes to learn from them?

How can so many Gods exist if everyone believes
that *their* God is the one and only?
Who says the book of their God is God's word?
What keeps people from writing about a fantasy
and calling it God's word?
How can people believe in a power that does no wrong,
when wrong is done?
Some believe the devil is at fault for all wrong.
But who hasn't once done something knowing it was wrong?
I say those who believe in such a power are just weak-minded people
looking for something to blame their sins on…
like the devil.
God does not exist.
   (3-12-1996)

Friendly Weather

People will come and people will go.
Not unlike a winter's snow.
Some will stay your whole life through.
But others may someday turn on you.
Watch yourself and beware of your "friends."
Because someday they may not make amends.
True friends are there forever.
Not just until there's a change in weather.
   (1-16-1997)

Dusk

The sun is setting, and with it, another day is gone.
The day of warmth and laughter that has lasted so long.
The night comes to play, with its star lit sky.
Peace comes to Earth, as the moon rises high.
The sky, so beautiful; the stars all a glow,
Guiding those watching, from far below.
   (1-21-1997)

The Party's End

The date for the party is set.
Everyone is invited, everyone is excited.
Party plans are seen to and the big day finally arrives.
Everybody you know is there, and everyone you don't.
The music is blearing through your body
as you begin the night you'll never forget.
The nightlife is taken to an extreme:
    There are kids having sex.
    There are kids drinking alcohol.
    There are kids smoking pot.
    There are kids doing drugs.
All still have their fun, but most with the help of such narcotics.

After the big bash, everyone returns home, dead tired.
Those who used, hung over.
Those who didn't, still all smiles from their happy memories.
Sunday comes and goes, and Monday brings school again.
The "big party" of the weekend is being talked about by everyone,
in good humor.
An announcement is suddenly made regarding that party night.
All humor and fun in the weekend has gone…
someone was killed.
Everyone got home from this party bash safely, but those two.
The most popular couple in school, killed in a car crash.
Though they are gone, they will never be forgotten.
Nor forgotten is the party night that turned sour.
    (3-27-1996)

On-going

Friends or foes,
who better knows,
of my sadness and my woes?
Is one really better,
than the other,
in times of weakened, saddened, splatter?
For time has come for you to do,
exactly what you need to.
Ignore the hype,
in spite of strife,
you may have, for your life.
   (4-2-1997)

Masterpiece

Sad but true,
who really knew,
that I had a crush on you?
I see you there,
your gorgeous hair,
flipping coaxingly in the air.
You close your eyes,
and I see inside,
the beauty that you try to hide.
It hurts my heart,
when you fall apart,
because you're a beautiful work of art.
   (4-8-1997)

Sleep

"Stay open," I tell my eyelids,
But they do not like to listen.
My lids droop further and further,
as I consciously try not to fall asleep.
But sleep invites me and beckons for me to fall to it.
It senses my presence and catches me as I fall.
   (4-10-1997)

View of a Tragedy

Romeo and Juliet, the love story of all time…
Where love springs from two families of a different kind.
And the rose, and its name, may smell so great;
But their love is forbidden by their own parents hate.
Hiding in a church, accepting their vows,
The two loves marry at the church minister's bow.
The kiss they give, after they tie that knot,
Defies their parents, and the war
Their families have fought.
But when death comes upon them,
as their blood is spilled,
With the loss of their children,
the two families' rivalry is healed.
   (4-21-1997)

Not What You See

If I love his eyes,
I'm only a looker.
If I love his body,
I'm simply a hooker.
If I need some attention,
I'm just a tease.
If I need a compliment,
I only want him to please.
All I want is to be,
The girl that I am.
And you'll say what you will,
but I'll still do what I can.
   (4-22-1997)

Growing Up

Candy drops in children's mouths.
Teddy bears that roam the couch.
Their dolls and toys protect the child,
Their stuffing temperaments' are never mild.
But once their child has gone away,
No longer do they hope to play.
   (6-4-1997)

Sorry

Why do people tell you they are sorry?
For it's only words that they say.
Actions speak louder than words of "I'm sorry."
Can't anyone understand?
People believe in forgiveness of every mistake
and misunderstanding.
I believe in denial and
I will never spring back like a rubber band.
   (8-26-1997)

Trinket

Love is a traveler of little fortune.
Cupid's arrow does not come straight for you.
The lover's path follows many twists and turns.
The darkness ahead only holds more dangers to learn.
   (9-9-1997)

Common Times

A sickness, a ravaging disease.
A plague that engulfs your entire body.
Stuffy and runny and red noses,
yuck, yuck, yuck.
Coughing and hacking and sneezing,
more and more snot!
Faintly being able to make out simple shapes.
Being drugged by cold medicine
that makes you pass out and fall to the floor.
Goodnight...zzz!
   (10-24-1997)

Close Minded

I don't know what happiness my future could hold anymore.
All that I have ever even wanted was to be happy.
Little kids are cruel, as I sometimes was.
I think that I'm now paying the price of being so snappy.
No one really knows what reflections their actions
will ripple.
No one really understands the feelings they attack.
No one knows how simple words can cripple.
No one knows what they do until they widen their insensitive crack.
   (8-26-1997)

Christmas Memories

When you close your eyes, in the dead of winter,
in the middle of the night,
You can see the Christmas tree and the presents it holds,
as you feel the warm fire and hear its crackling bite.
You remember the stories and the songs
You would hear and sing,
You remember having all of your family
under one roof again
and the love and feelings it would bring.
You can see the smiles and hear the laughter,
as we played our games.
So many people, having so much fun,
you hardly remember everyone's name.
And although you knew they would soon leave you
for another year, another day.
You simply enjoyed yourself, and now the memories,
as time ticks itself away.
    (11-16-1997)

Go Away

Stop looking at me,
I don't like to be stared at.
Just because I'm not you,
doesn't mean I'm a brat.
I know I look better,
than you, yourself do.
I've got their attention,
that's just too bad for you!
I know…it's just not fair,
I can wear spandex and elastic.
But don't you worry,
there's a surgery called "plastic."
You jealous little thing,
it's just so sad.
I know you wish you had my body,
you wish really bad!
    (4-22-1997)

Kira

Once in a land of white and snow, there lived Kira, the tiny Sprite.
She knows not of the treasures we hold, she only knows of the peril she fights.
For she has no home, no one to find, she is alone in the forests and night.
She can only dream of what human life is like, as do all little Sprites.
    (11-16-1997)

Making Faces

If only you could see into the minds
Of everyone around you.
What treasures you could behold.
So many secrets long forgotten,
and tales of truths untold.
   (12-2-1997)

Teresa Pope

The girl around the corner, someone we all know.
The friend we once loved, sometime long ago.
She is so innocent and so uncertainly sweet.
She is so lovely and so cute.
She was until we realized, that she's not what she seems.
Her face is no longer like a brightening gleam.
Her mood swings grow great,
And we're afraid to be near.
So now she's alone, betrayed by her own fear.
The mirror has two faces, so I have learned.
The friendship I once had, has now overturned.
When we were away from the crowd,
she was my friend again,
but soon we returned to life, and she would pretend.
She lies to herself, about who she truly is.
She dreams of fame and fortune, and all the show-bizz.
Her true friends have left, no longer wishing to play.
She does not notice, why must she live her life this way?
   (12-8-1997)

Politics

Tie the binds that fill the holes.
Hang the necks that speak the truth.
Stop those that achieve their goals.
Crack the places covered smooth.
   (3-17-1998)

Slowly

Once upon a quiet time,
I lived to be involved in life.
And now I drink the wine
that portrays my life without the strife.
Once the life has gone,
Once you are untouched,
Then you are alone
and life's no longer rushed.
   (2-16-1998)

Close

Close your eyes and feel the darkness
close in all around you. It creeps in and
closes your lungs with its tight grip.
Close to your heart, things are ripped away to
close the book on your life.
   (2-16-1998)

High

It's a shakedown of your nerves.
It's a meltdown of your brain.
It's a breakdown of your life.
It's a fun time to get High!
   (2-16-1998)

Understand

I am quite distraught, as my life currently stands.
I don't understand anyone.
I don't understand anything.
I don't understand why people insist
On shadowing the truth,
or hiding it completely.
I am so tired of being treated like an insignificant mouse.
I cry at night, but it does not sooth me.
Tears only bring questions into the eyes of the people who surround me.
Why are you crying?
What's the matter?
Do they not understand?
Are people really that stupid?
You must realize that your words hurt me, don't you?
Perhaps not.
Why else would you still be so cruel?
Why were you cruel in the first place?
I don't understand what I ever did to you.
Maybe I am the stupid one.
I just don't understand.
   (4-29-1998)

Do You Know?

I see you there.
Standing with that sly smile on your face.
You know.
You know that they exist.
You know the girls that will follow you,
and flirt with you.
You know you have a chance,
with any one of them.
You know they like you.
You know they want to be with you.
But do you know what I know?
I didn't think so.
   (5-1998)

Blink

There is
hidden meaning
in what you read right here:
Nothing is known in what you see—
Think to believe.
   (5-1998)

Refills

Some may see your

Glass as being half
empty. Pessimists.
Others may see it half
full. Optimists. Whatever
it may be, you still need
more juice.
   (5-1998)

Refreshment

Rain beat down on me.
Drops of dew are seeping threw
To my skin within.
   (5-1998)

The Cavity

The horrid loud, obnoxious sound
of grinding teeth echoes through your head.
The cavity is reeking havoc
on your poor, sensitive mouth.
The pains pulsate in time with the beat of your heart.
If only there were a dentist to be found.
   (7-18-1998)

Clockways

Tick, tock
Tick, tock.
That's what I hear.
Time is near,
dragging,
slowly,
endlessly,
on and on.
Tick, tock
Tick, tock.
The sound engulfs my mind.
Thoughts are cloudy
and rain comes from my eyes
down the streaked terrain of my face.
   (9-18-1998)

To Do You

To sleep, to dream
oh how I gleam
to wish, to go
oh you don't know
to be, so sexy
oh—you're only 16?
Oops…
   (2-13-2001)

Good Night

My eyelids have become, so,
…so heavy.
I can feel them…dr…dropping
…slowly dropping.
…closing…
closing to reveal
…heaven.
Heaven in…sl…sleep.
Sleepy heaven.
A complete collapse in consciousness.
Goodbye harsh light…good night.
Shall I see you in awhile?
After my nap.
Good night sweet light.
Good night sweet world.
   …good night.
   (9-21-1998)

Freeze Frame

Apparently I'm photogenic, or so they tell me.
I guess it's true.
There are few pictures of me that portray me
in a way other than happy,
with a huge smile on my face.
I wonder if my life really is the way it appears
in these frozen moments in time.
Do I have a good life?
Am I happy?
   (8-22-2000)

Josh

Just because my love for you
Over everything in the world
Shows you my secret and
Helps save my life from
Solitude doesn't permit
Anyone to put an
X over my mouth and shut me out!

Just me looking
over my
shoulder at the man who
helped give me life.
   (8-22-2000)

Know It

What if I told you my secret?
Could you handle it?
Would your emotion show regret?
   Could I handle that?
Read my eyes and read my mind...
   Can you handle what you find?
   (8-22-2000)

Diet Right

There's problems on the diet frontier.
I can't seem to get back to the body I once had.
The one I crave for, and miss.
I'm not motivated enough to exercise to excess,
but not strong enough to not eat either.
Motivation is what I need and strive for now.
I must…I must obtain a more beautiful self…
although I do sometimes fear my health.
I can't understand why society wants us
So skinny and boney.
All my life people have told me how skinny I was.
I have to hear it!
I'm not as pretty as I'd like to be,
so I made up for it in weight.
But now I'm losing even that.
It scares me.
I want people to look at me in awe of how I appear.
Not because I'm freakish, but only freakishly skinny.
I want others to be amazed at my tiny physique.
But much work must be done first.
   (2-11-2000)

Computers

AOL—www
.com
.org
How many mega bytes do you have?
Your bytes can BITE my shinny-metal-ass!
   (2-13-2001)

Classes

So close to freedom,
and yet—so far away.
Can't you let me go?
I do not want to stay!
Let me be far away
from your crazy behavior.
If only the clock moved faster
it would become my true savior.
   (2-13-2001)

Give it to Me Now

One boy-band, two boy-bands, three…
I don't want them. No.
I want the men.
The men of the world.
Where have they gone?
What are they doing?
If they're looking for something to do
and somewhere to go
my address is available
and I'm waiting at home.
 (2-13-2001)

Speed Racer

Time...
   Time...
      Time...
Why must you punish me so?
Go—go now—go faster.
Speed up—not slow down.
This is a fucking race
And I don't want to hear otherwise.
Just get the hell out of my sight!
   (2-13-2001)

Poetry

Something I once did, and then I missed
is coming back to me now.
Why did I let it go for so long, and let it go so far away?
How I missed you! Did you miss me?
So come to me now…freely, consciously, and willingly.
Come to the one that shed a tear for every day
you were away.
Wipe the streaks off my face and come back into me
…to complete me, once again.
   (2-13-2001)

Chapter 2:

Divine Guidance

If

If: the word of all deceptions.
If decides if something happens.
If is what you could have been,
if you want to do somethin'
But if you have no desire,
then if is not to be inspired.
    (4-11-1997)

One Thing

Who really knows where the answer lies?
Life is full of truths with drops and highs.
Once the beginning starts to become the end.
No one no longer feels the need to pretend.
The truth of life isn't one simple phrase.
For the truth of your life is a differential haze.
Being apart from the one thing you want,
Awakens your soul and opens your heart.
   (8-6-1997)

I Know

Who knows what evil lurks in the hearts of men?
Who knows what feelings linger in the hearts of friends?
I know that feelings can no longer be staged.
They know that my feelings are full of rage.
Who knows what feelings truly hide inside my heart?
I know what feelings tell me to do when we are apart.
Who knew that we could just let our feelings be?
No one knows what feelings you really have,
    Until you set them free.
    (8-5-1997)

Truth

The truth of your life isn't in the stars.
The truth of anything is hidden afar.
The truth of love isn't easy to take.
The truth of death is what you make.
   (8-8-1997)

Think

Look into your heart and find what it says.
Under the pain and joy lies the truth.
Keep trusting in the passion between your eyes.
Underestimating love is never how to go.
   (8-8-1997)

Dedication to Love?

Poor sweetheart,
I feel bad for you.
Your feelings are hurt,
and you don't know what to do.
I know how you feel.
I've been there myself.
But for you it's different,
you have all my help.
Whenever you need,
I'll be a friend for you.
If you feel like talking,
or want a shoulder to cry to.
But don't despair,
only time will heal.
Just always remember,
I know how you feel!
   (4-11-1997)

Trust

Distance is not to be feared in the entirety of the world.
Closeness is to be felt in the ruthless bitter cold.
Sweaty bodies writhe in the sweltering heat.
Trustfulness of the heart is what we long to keep.
   (8-8-1997)

Let Out

Boring, boredom in my mind.
Let us go; could you be so kind?
Raking, racking at my brain,
this thinking is such a bitter strain.
I want to go, to again be free.
I feel the struggle deep in me.
I need to leave, to go and fly.
Far from this, way up high!
   (4-4-1997)

Real

Our hearts can no longer be trusted,
for we are human, and our hearts will fail.
Only time will tell, when and if,
truth and love will prevail.
   (10-24-1997)

Voyage

Up and down the ladder's rungs of love.
Over and through the surging seas.
Through the boiling heats and blaze,
but never able to get over jealousy.
   (12-2-1997)

A Peaceful Night

The sun sets, and soon the moon rises.
Night has come once again.
Dark hits the earth with its gentle touch…
and I feel freedom come to my life.
All the pain and burdens of the day are gone.
Relaxation is welcomed as the stars peak out of the sky.
The summer air is warm and moist.
As the days clothes are lifted,
the night ones are applied.
Walking among the twinkling stars,
in the freedom of the night,
I feel at peace with myself.
Night is my time, my favorite time;
   This is the time for my thoughts.
The thoughts I have of the day…of life,
pour out freely just as the stars had done.
The night air is smooth…
smooth like the skin of someone's body.
The body is the holder of such thoughts,
like the night is the holder of all peacefulness.
Night brings peace once again.
   (3-11-1996)

Mindless

Palm trees stand inside my head.
Blue skies float above my brains.
Clear oceans swim in my eyes.
Green grasses grow in my hair.
Soft music flows through my voice.
Welcome to paradise in my life.
   (4-3-1997)

The Island

Chalk to chalkboard; pens to paper.
Inside thoughts flow softly through her.
Sometimes it's hard to let them shine,
because she has a one track mind.
Her mind so far away from here.
Somewhere warm and nice and clear.
Something she feels for this place,
could never, ever be escaped.
   (4-4-1997)

Why?

If you should enjoy life, why don't you?
If pleasure is a sin, why do you believe in heaven?
If life is a pleasure, you go to hell!
So why should you enjoy life?
What is its appeal?
   (1-14-1997)

Untitled

The time to be afraid has passed on.
The time to seize the moment is here,
but it won't be here long.
Front to front, the face is mine.
Never again will I fall behind.
Seize the day, don't run away.
Be the one that gets it done!
   (10-24-1997)

Life

Time has gone to spare no one.
Love is lost; all that's left is lust.
Seize the day to lead the way.
Close your eyes and picture the skies.
Fly away and forget today.
Live for yourself, and not for your health.
   (12-2-1997)

Turning Point

Happy Faces laughing hysterically over a simple oops
…spilled all over yourself.
A bit embarrassing, but enjoyable.
He knows, I think. Maybe.
Maybe not.
Who knows? Who cares?
It was fun. We have fun together.
Best buds, pals, chums, compadre.
"Now is the time you make your best friends."
Well, I know that I definitely enjoy his company.
   (10-21-1998)

Exploration Unknown

Relationship? Now?
Never.
I want to explore.
We are on the same wave link, him and I.
To explore, to have fun, to live our lives.
Friends who share their experiences,
share everything.
I can have fun.
Why?
Because I know what my future holds.
Where I will be, and who I will be with.
We have our fun now.
We will love each other when the time comes.
   (8-22-2000)

Love of Life?

What is love, if not for life?
Do people live to love?
Or do they love to live?
There would be no love without life...
   I do not know.
Why do people make love?
To give life?
Life must always come from love.
But why doesn't love always come from life?
What is love, if not for life?
   (1-8-1996)

The Game of Life

I sit on my porch;
I sit and I think.
About the things to come
and the things that now stink.
I sit on my ass
all God damn day.
But sometimes on the couch
I also lay.
You'd think I'm depressed
or maybe just sad.
But it's not that way,
I'm usually just mad.
Mad about things
I cannot change
Things I want
that are out of my range.
To far away
for me to find.
I sit on my ass
and I lose my mind.

Get off of your ass
you silly fool.
Get out in the world
and make them drool.
You can make them want you,
you know that you can.
It's just a matter
of knowing your hand.

What cards to play
and which ones to hold.
You cannot be taught
and you cannot be told.
Life is a game
you learn on your own.
Sometimes it sucks
but sometimes it's gold.
   (8-24-2001)

Chapter 3:

Love Worth Finding

Not Again

I hold not, you in my heart.
Fate keeps us far apart.
I see not, you in my dreams.
I hear the night's screams.
I feel not, your presence near.
I hold nothing that dear.
I hold not, yourself to mine.
My soul is slowly dying.
I know not, what happens now.
Fate delivers me when and how.
    (3-17-1998)

Layers

Happy now, why and how
Let it go, feelings show
No more tears, lessen fears
Work it out, scream and shout.

Miss you still, feelings real
No more sleep, thoughts are deep
Hug and kiss, hopeful wish
Emotions grow, now we know.

Show it true, just be you
Nothing fake, same mistake
Make it real, have to peel
Layers still, from free will.
   (1-14-2005)

Inside

Inside my heart, he beats hard and true.
Inside my head, he says "I love you!"
Inside my soul, he comes to stay.
Within my bed, do we lay.
Inside my hand, is his own.
Within the bed, love is known.
Inside his eyes, warmth comes through.
Within his heart, love shines true.
Inside this mirror of Mother Earth.
Within I feel all I'm worth.
   (12-21-1996)

Always

I see him there, his gorgeous face,
    His muscular body
He reaches for me and I could close my eyes;
    For I trust his touch.
He touches me and I am immediately lost
    Inside his arms.
I am his, now and always…
he could do anything he wanted with me,
    My love for him would never change.
He makes love to me; I feel his heartbeat
    Inside of my own.
Then, he holds me…and I know the
    Feeling of being safe.
I am in his arms, and I am safe.
It is here; here, where I always want to be
    Now and forever. Safe inside my love's arms,
    And inside his soul.
(11-6-1995)

What is It?

What is love? Will anyone ever know?
A person, perhaps a tree, maybe even snow.
I hate the snow, I live for heat; heat inside of me.
When that special someone stirs it up...
    With every touch of my body, heart, and soul.
I feel it now, and hope to feel it forever more.
He makes me smile, and makes me laugh...
I love him now and I'll love him always,
until the end of time.
(11-6-1995)

Sweetness in Love

"In a perfect world, I would never have a chance with her
because she deserves someone so much better.
But since this is a shitty world, maybe I have the slightest
little chance with someone like her."
This is what he wrote to my friend.
I never thought that any man could ever be
so sincerely sweet!
Unlike the last, who broke my heart,
this one does not use,
and I doubt if he would ever cheat!
I think that I am falling for him, but it just feels so strange.
He's like my best friend.
He was never before in the "lovers" range.
I feel so good, that he is so sweet.
He has never once, treated me bad.
Not even when I bitched at him because, for some reason,
I was really mad.
All of my friends say that he cares for me,
and that he has never wanted anything more than this.
I do believe, that I am falling for him,
and can hardly wait for that very first kiss!
   (5-1-1996)

Counting the Days

Day 1: I told him yes. I think he never would have guessed.
So now we're together, hopefully forever.

Day 2: He stayed with me after school. He's so sweet to me, he makes me feel like a fool.
He grabbed my hand, but with quite a good demand.
I very much enjoyed, his little ploys.

Day 3: He kissed me…almost surprising enough for me to die.
But I never felt so loved before…I wonder why.

Day 4: We went out to many places, all quite quaint.
Every time we sat down, he put his arm around me; I felt like I could faint.
He bought me 2 roses, a pink and a red.
He also, so sweetly, kissed my forehead.
He smelled so good, I could eat him alive!
Every time he kissed me, I felt I melted inside.

Day 5: Last night, I swear, was like a dream.
Today I awoke, all smiles, my face simply a beam!
I honestly think that I have found the right one!
Never in one night, like the last, have I had so much fun!
    (5-6-1996)

Together

Two loves come together, to closely become one.
In the night and in the bed, they cuddle
With the one they call "hun."
He holds her tightly and close to him, closely to his heart.
This feeling of love and safety will stay forever with her,
even when they are apart.
His arms are wrapped around her, to protect her,
and with love.
It's as though they and their love, have been blessed
from high above.
And as he sleeps she watches him,
with love filling her eyes.
She's never seen anything as beautiful as him,
cradling her in his arms.
As she dozes off happy and content,
he awakes to her motionless body,
in the bed where love is meant.
Her body is so relaxed and she feels so warm
against his skin.
He takes her love for him, and her beauty,
and breaths it deeply in.
Their love together is stronger than any machine
or a million men.
Their love will last as long as forever can.
   (11-11-1996)

Love Under Keeping Eyes

What do your eyes hide from the world they watch?
What do my eyes hide from the life that they live?
What do our souls feel way down deep inside?
Why do our lips tremble at the passions that they give?
  (8-8-1997)

Mine Only

I am no slut, no whore!
I do not have 100s of lovers stashed around the world.
I do not need them.
I have one man, and only one.
He is who I love, who I trust, and who I make love to.
There is no one else. No one else.
And now I am torn from even him.
Now there is no one at all.
I hold him so close to my heart,
but yet he still feels so very far away.
I can look into his eyes and see the love he has for me,
only me, as I feel for him.
Though everyone may not believe in true love
because of what they may have experienced, I do.
I believe that true love does exist,
although I may not have before.
I also now believe in true friendship.
Friends who will stay until the end.
Friends who have been emotionally there for me,
even though they could not always be physically there.
And they know that I am no slut...I do not share my body.
I am no whore...I do not sell my body.
All I am is a lover.
One single solitary lover to one other single solitary lover.
That is what I am.
I have found my love, my life.
Perhaps others should start looking for theirs,
rather than paying attention to my lover, my friends,
and my life.
Find your own, for this one is mine and mine alone!
   (9-23-1996)

To My Friend
Dedicated to Lydia Hall

I have a friend, who is the best of them all.
She is there when I turn around,
and catches me when I fall.
We are tighter than atoms packed closely together.
We are friends forever, no matter the weather.
We share everything that you could possibly
want to count.
We buy each other gifts, no care for their amount.
We both love all animals, especially our cats.
But our relationship goes further, and deeper than that.
Most don't understand the love we have for each other.
The love for our friendship, that stays, now and forever.
She has become my family, she's like a sister to me!
We will be together as friends forever,
living life to be free!
 (1-21-1997)

Lydia

Love: Something you have for your friends and they have for you.

Youth: Something that will stay forever in your actions and always in your appearance.

Devotion: Something you have in everything you do.

Intelligence: Something you have more of than you realize, or want to admit.

Awesome: Something you will always be in my mind.

(1-27-1997)

First Kiss

I close my eyes, and what do I see?
I see my best friend, staring back at me.
We go off and roller blade, like we always do
How could he know that I want to tell him, "I love you"?
I hide my feelings in the life that I live.
If he only knew what I had to give.
But my life is separate from his own.
He answers to the voice of a different tone.
As I live my life, and he lives his,
I can only dream of a true love kiss.
   (8-5-1997)

You Are

My love has taken leave away for certain days of three.
And so the feelings I gaze, are finally cast upon thee.
For you are my love, of the heart and of the soul.
You make the days a-bright, and make my tensions cool.
But hence when my love returns to what is his,
To my Truth and Soul I will leave only this…
Fear not what is unknown,
    To your mind and your heart.
Fear only of the pain,
    Of true love's part.
    (8-6-1997)

True Love

I heard the sound and immediately rushed to the window.
There he was, coming to see me.
Without a word, I knew why he was here;
he told me in his eyes.
Without a flinch, he picked me up
and carried me to my bedroom.
The door closed softly behind us.
He kissed me, so tenderly,
I could feel his love all around me.
Without a sound, my robe gently fell to the floor,
followed by his clothes close behind it.
Without any other care in the world,
he laid me on my bed,
as lovingly as could be.
Without asking, he knew exactly where to touch me,
to make me feel safe.
He kissed me in every spot that had true love
hidden deep inside.
Then with all his love, he made love to me,
knowing I would show my love in return.
And without a thought but me,
he held me tight and told me exactly
what I wanted to hear:
"I love you," he said, and vowed always to be mine.
   (2-26-1996)

Made for One

The man I see, I've seen before.
But now I feel like I want him more than ever.
His eyes, those gorgeous eyes stare back at me.
It's like he knows my thoughts.
The thoughts I have, of him, of us.
I can see them shinning back in his eyes.
His lips, so precious, so delicate.
How I wish they weren't so far away.
His hands, so strong, but their touch so gentle.
How I wish they were around me.
His body, so tense, but somehow, so relaxed.
How I wish it was close to my own.
He looks at me, but in a way he never has before,
almost like there was love in his eyes.
I smile. He smiles back at me and slowly walks over.
He stops, just inches away.
So close he is, but still seems so far.
His hands touch my face, and I feel as though
they have always belonged there.
Then his lips touch my own, with great passion,
but still as gentle as can be.
His eyes, those gorgeous eyes, disappear behind the lids.
Just as mine had done.
His body, pressed so tight to mine.
Nothing could feel so safe or more right.
The kiss he gives me, so incredible, so loving, so real.
I feel like melting in his arms.
Our hearts seem to beat in perfect sync.
Our lips, our bodies, our minds, our souls…
All simply made for one…
each other.
   (3-5-1996)

Lust

Now is the time, to let my love shine.
To show him my love, and give him a hug.
To show him I care, that I'll always be there.
To give him that kiss, on those sweet tender lips.
He knows I'm not shy, and for him, I would die!
   (4-18-1997)

Sacred Secrets

Where no one else sees, his arms are around me.
I may be elsewhere spoken for, but I don't mind.
We have never let our desires flow,
so the sexual tension between us thrives inside.
If I could touch his sweet lips to mine just once,
I would truly know how I feel.
An affair would be our sacred secret,
and only to us, would it truly be real!

So close to my skin, my blood is moved
By his gentle breath.
Our eyes lock in temptation, our wills weaken in strength.
Our hands barely touching, the feelings will flow.
My mind on him alone, only he and I shall know.
   (5-27-1997)

Where to Look

If only she knew who to go to, if only
She knew what she wanted.
The man she loves, the man that has loved her
for her entire life, stands before her,
but sometimes she does not even notice him.
In her heart she knows that she truly does love this man,
but the feeling she has in her stomach
makes her look towards another.
This other, is so different from the one she knows and loves.
She only needs to blink to picture his every detail.
His tall and slender, but muscular body.
His short brownish-blonde hair,
every intricate detail of his face...
the line his lips make when he speaks,
the blink of his long lashes with those unforgettable eyes,
the smile on his face.
She cannot put it out of her mind.
But still she knows she is wrong.
Why would such a man,
one capable of having any woman he wanted,
want this poor little waif?
Why would such an incredible man,
want such an ugly little girl?
Even though she knows she wants him,
her heart makes her behave.
And so, every time he walks by and smiles at her...
she can only pretend to know what it would be like
to press her lips to his...just once.
   (10-24-1997)

Picture Perfect

And so the truth is finally revealed to me.
Although I may love this man I am with,
I have become no longer infatuated with him.
It puzzles my every being as to how
I could be so heartless
to stay with a man that loves my every fiber and being,
when I no longer see the need to have his body,
as I once did.
His friendship will forever be mine, and so mine is his.
But I no longer wish to pursue my life
as one man's destiny.

I was once told a very interesting story.
It had me picture a man I wanted,
but perhaps didn't even know.
I did not picture my lover, but instead pictured another.
He appeared in my mind and did not leave
even when my love tried to force him away.
He will not leave my thoughts,
as I fear he has always been there hiding.
But hide no longer he will; he opens himself to me.
He appears around every corner of my mind,
as though I shall not be rid of his influence on my life.
He will never in truth know as to how I feel,
but soon I will give myself to his thoughts
as our inner spirits lock and embrace each other
for all time.
    (10-29-1997)

Chance

He looks at me, I look at him,
   And suddenly I knew.
He was the one, the only one,
   That could make my heart one, not two.
I've been hurt before, the feeling is still fresh,
   Deep inside my heart.
I should leave this place, for fear of hurt,
   But my legs would not depart.
My life was empty, but now, somehow,
   He put me in his trance.
Take a chance girl, go on,
   Just take the chance.
   (11-6-1995)

Derek's Eyes

Swimming in an ocean of blueness.
Their stare suddenly relieves your stress.
It sends tingles through your body
to be locked in sight with his eyes.
Never before had you noticed their beauty.
Every blink, all the more than the last,
what a delightful surprise.
   (1-13-1998)

Ira

Inner thoughts beg for
Reality to flow
   Again.
Radian light
As a presence is shown.
   Deliciously delivered and
    Kept in mind, and in
      Your heart.
(1-26-1998)

Man of Your Dreams

Walk. Walk slowly, in slow motion.
See. See his eyes embrace your own.
The background vanishes to nothingness.
Blackness engulfs the two, but you can see.
A dream-like state of confusion and peace.
The blur that is him grows nearer.
The two bodies stop in silence.
Each hand is lifted to touch that of the other.
He reaches for your hand, and you for his.
The fingertips touch softly.
His palm mirrors your own.
Sudden noise backs them apart.
The background is replaced,
and you walk on by the man of your Dreams.
   (1-26-1998)

A Reality Instinct

Strange things have been happening in my mind.
There are so many people that I would like
To be better friends with,
or lovers, perhaps.
I had the opportunity, to become a lover,
a one-night stand, but chose to decline.
He laid with me at night, cuddled close.
It felt relaxing and warm, yet somehow,
unnerving and frightening.
I did not think of him, my mind was nowhere near our bodies,
but flying far away.
My mind flashed me pictures of my past lover.
I felt as though I missed him, and his presence.
But it faded away.
Then I thought of another, one I have known for so long,
but barely know at all.
His look has power, a captive power
that holds in your mind long after the last time you met.
And so his presence embraced me that night,
and stayed long after,
until the next night fell.
I could feel his arms around my body
and his sweet, slow, erratic breath moving gently on my face.
His touch unlike that of the one I currently laid with,
unlike any I've ever known.
Unlike the movies portray, and unlike sweet dreams at night.
Unlike reality could ever be,
   Unlike life.
   (1-26-1998)

Smile

Night time.
Sometime, long ago.
I saw the way you loved me.
Your eyes,
entwined to mine.
Our hearts,
locked in time.
Our bodies,
close together.
Our souls, a pair,
forever.
    (3-17-1998)

Insanity

Four days ago.
Four days from two years.
It would have been, at least.
Two years with the man of my dreams.
The man I loved.
The man who loved me, who held me.
I don't know why I left him.
What was I seeking?
Freedom, I think.
But freedom from what?
From my love?
From my life?
I made a mistake, one unlike any other.
A mistake that I will pay for, forever.
If only he knew,
If only he knew.
I miss you.
I love you.
   (5-4-1998)

To Be

I wish I could see or know what it is that I wanted.
I want to be held, to be admired.
To be told I'm beautiful during the day.
To be kissed on the neck at night.
To be held the night through when I shake
and tremble with fear.
To have the tears from my eyes wiped away
by a sweet, loving hand.
To be alive.
To not be alone.
To be cared about enough to want to live.
To be.
   (7-10-1998)

Bed Flirts

Giggles.
A laugh.
A serious look.
"Stop that."
"Stop what?"
"Boy…that's my ear lobe!"
"I know."
A sigh.
More giggles.
"That tickles."
A smile.
A caressing tongue.
"Girl…that's my neck."
"I know."
A look.
Two smiles.
A passionate kiss.
   (6-12-1998)

Perfectly You

The feeling I get when those undigested chunks
pass through my throat on their journey
to the lonely porcelain bowl
is the feeling I get when I see you.
It may be painful at first,
but it makes you feel better in the end.
I want to be beautiful for you.
You are so perfect in the way you carry yourself.
I want to be perfect too.
Perfectly skinny, and perfectly beautiful.
Because I need to be perfect…
If I want you.
   (7-10-1998)

Only When Heaven Knows

She looks dead, laying face down,
sound asleep on her white sheets.
But she is quite alive, and aware.
His kiss of her exposed neck
startles her from her sound sleep,
but she is happy.
She rolls over to face the sweet,
smiling face above her.
He brushes his soft hand through her hair,
ever so gently, then caresses her cheek.
She smiles at the feeling it gives her:
the feeling of safety, though he is only here shortly.
He lays next to her wrapping her in his strong,
warm arms.
His tongue slips sweetly and slowly
to hers in an unearthly kiss.
But he only holds her tightly in his arms.
His hands do not move down her body.
She enjoys his safe company,
even if only for a little while.
   (7-10-1998)

Feeling Fresh

Feeling fresh, awakened and anew
I hope you feel the same way too.
I can't believe it took so long
To figure out what went wrong.
We both put up a great big wall
I'm glad you bumped me in the hall.
You make me smile and make me feel
something great that I know is real.
   (1-14-2005)

Chemistry Homework?

We met, a while ago, in a common place.
In this class, hard and long.
Chemistry it was, boring and outdrawn.
First day, group project:
Say hello to those around.
...hello, Hello, HELLO, hello...
Next class, I chanced sitting near.
It was good I did.
We've talked, had lunch, studied together since.
A friend asked me before, Boyfriend material?
But absolutely not at all, at least not at the time.
Now I'm not so sure.
Three hours last night,
two the night before,
we spent together working on our "chemistry,"
derogatory or not.
Last night, this morning, my face all smiles,
unusual for a test day.
But I'm happy.
Could there be good chemistry in my own future?
   (9-25-1998)

Presence

Sex isn't something that people take lightly,
until you're in love.
So head over heels in love that you periodically smile,
just because.
How long, how good, how sexually satisfying...
not quite as important as once thought.
But...how passionate...
each lock of your lips trapped in time.
How intense...
so much so that you shake and tremble.
How you've never before felt so complete.
You can close your eyes,
breath in deeply,
feel their presence...
and you smile...just because.
   (4-7-1999)

My Best Friend

He's not here, where could he be?
Sad really...
sad that I sit and wait to spend time with him...
but only as friends.
We've been friends for years now,
but it's no longer the same.
I remember how I've wanted to kiss him since he came.
He constantly appears dancing in my head.
We'll be doing our project and our eyes will meet.
Our lips will finally join for the kiss I have longed for,
deep and sweet.
This is the fantasy that plays in my head...
over and over.
I've wanted for so long for him to become my lover.
But as it now is, we are just friends, best friends.
He has a hook-up somewhere else; I pray for their end.
I want him to come to me, and know how I feel.
He will make love to me, and know that it's real.
   (5-1-2000)

Juicy Words

I have recently expressed my love to my man.
But today my mind strays.
I can't seem to understand my mood on this strange day.
I feel irritable and unruly,
snapping at people for insignificant things.
Perhaps the part of me that is petrified is trying
to catch up to the part that is perfectly content.
I fell in love with him, and it now terrifies me.
I have told him I love him, and I feel as though I do,
but I deny it to myself.
I think...maybe, if I don't admit to myself
That I am vulnerable,
and in love, that I won't get hurt.
I know that I'm not being true to my heart.
He has, in his own way, expressed that he feels the same.
How can I know if he's truthful?
For he has yet to say those *three little words*.
Days ago, I told him "Olive Juice,"
a grade school ploy that was used to tell someone
"I love you."
"Olive Juice too," he replied to me.
It put a smirk on my face, but not for long.
I realize it's not the juice I want from him,
I want the comfort of being loved,
and the confidence it gives to be told so.
   (2-16-1999)

Hope of a Friend

He's one of my best friends, my confident.
He knows every intimate detail of my history
with the opposite sex.
Every problem, every triumph I had with the last,
is somewhere in his memory bank.
His mistakes, his rewards, are somewhere
locked in my mind.
I want to tell him my aspirations.
What I hope and what I dream.
He is my best friend.
But how do I tell my best friend that I love him?
   (8-22-2000)

Understanding True Love

Are there words that can really describe true love?
Does true love really even exist?
It is beauty, truth, and life all combined into one.
It is something that should be known
to the depths of one's soul;
Something you live and breath and feel.
Not something in your head, or even in your heart,
But something that is part of you.
Like breathing is a part of life, and healing a part of pain.
It is not the thought of it or the touch,
But the understanding.

Understanding this makes one truly whole
and truly alive.
But for most, like me, and like you,
this truth will never be known,
never be held as the most important aspect of life.
As something so pure
And so innocent
As it should Be.
   (8-22-2001)

Four Letters

Single and swinging, this is the life; or is it?
Most of the time I'd say it could be.
Not tied down; committed to no one.
But why not now?
It's been almost a year.
I like it, I love it, and I definitely want some more of it.
But what else?
I miss the love…being loved.
Being held after intimate relations,
someone telling me how beautiful I am,
and how much they love having me around.
But not only that,
how much they love me.
Life can be fun…
but it's so less enjoyable without that
one little four letter word.
   (2-13-2001)

The Perfect Friend

A new love has come into my life. He is my best friend.
I learned, he has liked me for over six months,
even when my heart belonged to another.
But now that the old love is gone, he has taken the chance
and asked me.
I was flattered he liked me, but still to crushed by the old love's
cheating heart and lying ways.
But this new love never stopped trying for me.
The thing that made me change my mind
was what he wrote to a friend:
"If this were a perfect world, I would never have a chance with her,
because she deserves someone so much better.
But since this is a shitty world, maybe I have the
smallest chance to be with her."
I never thought that any man could be so utterly sweet!
When I learned this, I think I almost cried!
He has always been sweet to me.
Never once in the entire time we've been friends, has he yelled at me.
Not even when I accidentally blew up at him because I was
mad at something else.
So now, I am dating my best friend.
A man who has cared for me through everything I have been through
and has always been there for me.
I feel so strange dating someone I only thought of as friends,
just a little while ago.
But I enjoy his company more than ever now.
And I know, that no matter what happens,
we will always be there for each other.
Through thick and thin, through good times and bad;
we will never stop being the very best of friends.
   (5-2-1996)

Sunshine

I have not seen, a sunshine beam
From your face, at this place.
You are missed as much as your kiss.
Hold me tight, it's right tonight.
Cuddling close together, can we stay forever?
Missing you when you're gone,
Thinking of our favorite song.
You are dancing in my head,
Can we please now go to bed?
   (1-14-2005)

Just Because

Just because it isn't obvious,
doesn't mean it's not true.
Just because I don't say it,
doesn't mean
I'm not thinking it.
Just because you know who I am,
doesn't mean you know me.
Just because you're in my past,
doesn't mean you'll be in the future.
Just because my heart screams for you,
doesn't mean I have to listen to it.
    But I want to.
    (8-22-2000)

Chapter 4:

Opposites Attract

No More

Alright now, that is it!
Enough of this bullshit.
No more boys, no more lies.
No more feeling like I have to cry.
No more wanting, no more waiting.
No more love, no more hating.
No more tears and no more pain.
No more comfort, just less sane.
No more smiles and no more trust.
No relationships, only lust.
   (1-24-2005)

Answers Await

I want to tell him, he should know.
I fell for him, but he let me go.
There are no men, only boys,
And they expect that we're their toys.
This is not how it works, sad to say.
Treat her like this, she will not stay.
I can't believe I await his reply
He is so sorry, but doesn't know why.
Sitting here, I feel like shit.
I thought that he could take the hint.
He makes me wait another day.
My feelings have gone astray.
There isn't time to forget the pain,
Only the tears remain.
I cried for you, I can't believe.
You are my biggest pet peeve.
Knowing nothing about real life,
You are too young, too full of spite.
Learn someday, what I now know.
You say stay, but I have to go.
    (1-12-2005)

Love Dream

Just thought I'd drop you a little line to say hello.
(To my fake boyfriend.)
Do you have any idea how much I love you?
(And how much I wish you loved me back.)
I miss you so much when we're apart.
(Which is always.)
At night I think of you sneaking into my room
and kissing me on the cheek.
(Fantasy coming up.)
I awake to your smiling face and you hold me
The entire night.
(Just like my teddy bear.)
You tell me how beautiful I am
as you run your fingers through my hair.
(Grr…caught on the bedpost again.)
I think I would die without you here to protect me.
(Coming to my funeral tomorrow?)
    (7-10-1998)

You're Free

Wondering alone in the dusk.
How lonely this place has become.
The feeling of love has gone.
The joy of life in none.
Your touch on my skin, but a whisper.
Your voice in my head, but a brush.
The warmth of your presence, now coldness.
The safety of embraces, now broken.
The blur of the colors, not known.
Your heart, not mine, not owned.
   (3-17-1998)

Used

Used is how I feel, I only want to die!
The man I loved betrayed me forever,
   Just to be macho with his friends.
I loved him, but now I know that he never
   Loved me in return.
I never thought I would see the day
when we would not make amends!
He broke my heart in a million pieces!
But the thing is, he doesn't even care.
Even though he had always promised to protect me,
   He said he'd always be there!
What will I do? Where will I go?
   His face is everywhere I look!
But I can never forget, never let go
Of the trust he betrayed,
   That he so cowardly took.
This man, I thought, I would love forever,
   And he would love me.
   I even let him take my virginity!
Now I flinch, at even the thought of him,
   Being in the same proximity!
The first one I let myself love, in such a long, long time.
   How could he be so cold?
He broke my heart, so I broke it off.
   Never did I think I would, or even could,
   Have ever been so bold.
He seems so amused,
   That he knows I am used!
   (4-24-1996)

Hold Me

Hold me.
Grip me tight.
Pull me closer.
I'm afraid.
Keep me warm.
It's cold.
Protect me.
I feel safe.
Let me relax.
I want to.
But don't leave.
I'll be alone.
Hold me close.
That's right.
But don't love me.
Just let me go.
   (6-12-1998)

It is You

Love isn't what you make of it.
Love is what it makes of you.
For when the truth comes around,
Love is what you already knew.
But once love turns to hate,
Your love of life is what's betrayed.
   (8-8-1997)

Wanting

I don't know what else to do.
My life seems so empty.
I'm so lonely.
I'm so drained.
I'm so in love with him.
I want him in my life.
I want to feel his breath on my face.
I want to feel his lips on my own.
I need to feel his arms around me in one single embrace.
I need you!
I need to look at your smile, your gorgeous face,
your massive hands that would protect me
…if only you loved me.
I lost when I lost you.
I never had my chance.
I never had that kiss.
I never had you.
   (8-9-1997)

Chasing the Chances

When I was a little girl,
I only wanted one thing when I grew up:
to have a man that loved me, to spend my life with.
Now I'm beginning to wonder if this is really that realistic.
I've dated guys and now have someone steady,
someone I love.
But suddenly something inside me makes me
want something new.
I may love him, I do!
But I feel as though I have missed the excitement
of the chase and the chance.
I suppose I'm probably lucky to have this man by my side.
I only wish I knew what it would be like to be single again.
What if it was wonderful?
What if men actually thought about me in a way
other than "his woman"?
I wouldn't be someone so far gone.
I would be a girl that was available.
But would it matter?
Perhaps if I were single again, I wouldn't like it at all.
The men wouldn't flock to me
like they do to the models in the movies.
They would turn and run faster than I could blink.
   (10-24-1997)

Virus

As the virus of the flu makes its way through my system,
My sleep reveals the man that I love.
He stands in my head, and in my heart.
The one I think I love, but the one
that I do not make love to.
If only I knew how he felt.
If only I knew how I felt.
Maybe then I would know what felt right.
   (8-5-1997)

Love of a Lifetime

Where must I go to have the love of a lifetime?
Where must I go to get the love of a lifetime?
Where must I go to get the love I have,
that love, my love; the love of a lifetime?
I am here, far away from my love, but why?
He is there, far away from his love, but why?
Why must we be separated?
So far away.
I want him here; I want him now.
I want him here with me.
To have our love, to make love.
I need to do that, for he is apart of me.
For him to be here, here with me,
would be the greatest gift of all eternity!
    (1-11-1996)

Love is...

There are no real happy endings to every story.
Inside the soul we feel the pains of what is lost.
Once upon a time love was simple and easy.
But when the modern days reach you,
you know the pains at all costs.
Even if someone truly loves you, for all you're worth,
doesn't mean you find a happy ending in your life.
Because the truth stings much worse than any fairy tail.
The truth of love will never be found,
no matter how much we would like!
(8-9-1997)

Check Please!

Once upon a time I fell in love.
Time after time I thought about him.
Not my love, my life...
he is not bombarded by my mind's haze.
The one who resides in my heart
Has love way below truths rim.
But the one I love does not return that love, not to me.
He has found another while I was finding him.
   (8-9-1997)

Gone Away

I don't know what to do.
I'm not sure where to turn.
I need to tell someone,
of the love that I yearn.
I know that he likes me,
and I know that he cares.
But I'm not really sure,
how long he will be there.
He says he will protect me,
he tells me not to worry.
But I fear one day,
he may leave in a hurry.
   (4-22-1997)

How Does it Make You Feel?

Do you know what you feel?
That pain, way down deep inside…
It's love, but it's a bad thing.
It's evil, destructive, and never forgiving.
So why do we long for it so?
You never truly know what love is.
You can't see it, hear it, or taste it.
But you can feel it.
Not with your fingers or body,
but with your soul.
How does it make you feel?
   (12-2-1997)

Hope Bleeds

There once was a girl with hope in her heart.
There once was a time when she believed.
Then life dealt her cards that broke her apart.
And now she dies inside because her heart bleeds.
(1-11-1998)

Te Quiero

A Spanish serenade to a loved one.
Far beneath her window he sits,
professing his love for her.
The wind is softly blowing through the cool night air.
A single tear drops and falls from her eye
as she rejects him.
But he does not leave.
He continues to try and win her love with all of his might.
"Remember all the times, all the love, the life we shared?"
But she does not care.
His heart is broken and cries out in pain for his lost love.
   (5-1998)

A Little Ditty

Look there. Did you see?
He was looking at me!
Sweet baby you look so lonely.
Like a little lost puppy that came home with me.
How I wish I could show you why.
You know you get me oh so high.
Where do you hide?
Where do you go?
Where do you live?
Why don't you know?
   (10-24-1997)

An Empty Bed

An empty bed, with empty sheets.
How depressing.
If only I could have it.
That one thing: to be held.
The touch of a friend,
Perhaps not even a lover.
The warmth of his body near.
The safety of his embrace.
The feel of his breath on your neck,
and the sound that it makes.
A bed no longer empty.
A girl no longer lonely.
If only it were true for me.
   (6-12-1998)

Words Speak Louder than Thoughts

So I thought I knew him;
I thought that I had some clue.
I was so wrong about everything,
but now I know what I do.
I know.
I attract the players,
the geeks,
and the losers.
Why? How?
How do I get so lucky?
Is it my looks, the way I flirt?
Do they think I'm a slut?
What do they think?
Or do they think at all?
Do I think?
Think before I act?
I don't, I know.
I wish I would, or could.
Perhaps even if I could think a little
before I opened my big mouth.
What comes out of my mouth?
Does it even matter?
Words don't speak my mind.
They're opposite of each other.
Opposite.
Opposites attract.
Think of things I could do.
If only I knew, knew what it was,
or is, that I want.
I don't know.

I only know when it's not something I want.
Then I know.
I know it hurts me,
Deep down inside.
And the tears fall, and drop,
silently on the sheets.
   (9-18-1998)

No More Boys

As I sit here I realize,
there's no real reason for surprise.
We know they're pigs and women are bitches,
just looking for the riches.
But it is not true for me, for you,
because they are looking too.
I cannot believe what I know;
my sadness and tears will grow.
Why can't I find a real man?
No more boys, "Ah God damn!"
They have no knowledge, no life skills,
and it kills.
So young and new, they're babies too,
but we're expected to coo?
What is wrong? Why do I care?
Run your fingers through my hair.
Protect us from the world's great dangers.
But still I am angered.
I cannot have, I cannot hold.
How many times must you be told?
We require more than men do,
and I know it's tricky for you.
Read my mind; look in my eyes.
Take away my terrible cries.
    (1-12-2005)

Lust

Lust.
That's all it is.
I want you…
near me,
with me,
in me.
Nothing more.
Well, I suppose…let's cuddle.
Hold me.
Caress me.
Kiss me.
Make love to me.
No!
Have sex with me.
Do not involve me with…
    …with love.
I do not love.
I cannot.
Love hurts me,
injures me,
leaves me.
I do not want love.
I want you.
   (6-12-1998)

Chapter 5:

Desert Desolation

Without Help

One simple, sad blink
of her long, pale lashes
sends a drop of water
on a tumbling journey
down her pink cheek.

Why does she hurt so?

Days are filled with
a deafening silence
that pounds into her head
like a canyon avalanche
has toppled onto her.
Nights are filled with
the saddening sounds of
salty sobbing tears
that soak her sheets.

Why does she stay miserable?

Her days want to be filled
with a joy that will brighten
her eyes and her heart.

Why does she do nothing?

She cannot reach the light,
to let its sweet, warm rays
into her life.

Why is she alone?

Her world
is permanently
dark and cold,
night and day.
No way out.
Without help.
　(6-19-1998)

Watered Down

Blood is thicker than water, or so they say.
Blood is salty and strained in its word.
Water is pure. Rushing or calm, water is always peaceful.
But to some, the thought of their own blood is peaceful.
I am beginning to believe in the fact
That releasing this thickness
may in-fact release you.
Water is clear, pleasing to look at, or through
...almost heavenly.
Blood is dark, painful to release, and almost devilish.
Perhaps this is why the release of blood releases tension,
stress, and pain.
But what happens when the release of that pain
only turns to more pain?
What happens when your blood runs dry?
When the once plentiful flow suddenly stops
...what then?
Water will flow forever and replenish itself.
Water may be thinner than blood,
but it will never run dry!
Once blood runs dry, that burden, that pain,
ceases to exist.
   (9-23-1996)

Bad Morals

Water drips…it rips and grips your mind.
Wind blows…it hurries up the time.
Sun shines…it scorches and burns your skin.
Pain hurts…it pokes and prods within.
Life drags…it goes on, and lacks in fun.
Hope fades…because you are loved by none.
 (2-13-2001)

Cruel Darkness

The hallway is dark, but there is still light to be seen.
I see no one and I know I am alone,
No one feels the pain as I do.
    No one else can see.
The pain of life that I know,
    No one else knows quite like me.
They play their jokes and have their fun,
    All at my expense.
They can't feel the hurt inside of me,
    They don't care how much.
It gives them pleasure to see my pain,
    my weaknesses, my crutch.
But I still feel good inside of me;
    There is always light before you break.
Maybe someday, they will realize,
    The error of their mistake.
    (11-6-1995)

Listen Up

He never listens to a single thing I say.
    He screams and yells and tells me to shut up
and listen to what he says I said.
He tells me lies, so far from the truth,
    I can tell, he never listens.
He doesn't care about anything I do,
    Because he never listens to what I say.
To him, he's always right, never wrong.
    I am always wrong because he's always right.
He says "Change your attitude, I don't like it."
Excuse me,
    But I'm not the one that is being sarcastic, unfair,
    And not listening.
He thinks I'm still a little kid, and won't let me grow up.
    Maybe that's why he never listens.
Whoever said that kids should be seen
and not heard anyway?
    I'm not a kid! If only he would listen,
if only he would see!
But he never listens to what I say.
    He *never* listens to *me*!
    (12-12-1995)

Blindness

Left out and lost amongst the crowd.
Though surrounded by people, friends and foes,
   I still feel alienated.
All alone, by myself, sitting next to someone I know,
   But who doesn't know me.
I look again, and I see all those people,
   None of which see me in return.
It's like they're blind;
blind to the world I see and understand.
I understand what's happening.
   I see the death of a world amongst us.
   (1-8-1996)

To Be Happy

All my life, I've only wanted one thing…
to be happy.
Through all my life, I've never achieved that one thing…
to stay happy.
Everyone around has problems bigger than mine…
I help them…
they are happy.
No one pays attention to my problems.
No one bothers to help me…
    I am not happy.
If only once someone would listen to just me,
without turning all the grief on their problems.
They start out helping me, but then
they become more important…
they need to be happy first.
And I am too weak not to help them,
I want them to be happy.
Even though I know…
    I will never be happy.
    (2-20-1997)

Wet

Love is playful inside of my heart.
And there it stays,
though my heart breaks apart.
All those around have strewn their problems upon me.
Now with all this weight, I become weak in the knees.
The stress inside just builds to a boiling high.
I stand alone in their rain, while they stand dry.
   (12-17-1996)

Where?

Being there, that strange yet somehow familiar place,
I began to get chills all over.
Not just through my spine, but literally all over.
I don't know what to do.
This place is so familiar, but still somehow, so very cold.
The people here, the are my friends, but they seem so far away.
Could I be imagining this awful experience?
But it's not just in my mind.
I reach out for comfort, but I touch nothing.
They are so far away. I feel so alone.
Why? Why would I want to be here?
I'm a stranger.
But I do! I want to stay!
There is something, something that is driving me away, so far away.
Away where it is so cold and very friendless.
    (1-9-1996)

Betrayed

Betrayed I am, for my love is lost.
    He betrayed my trust, sparing my feelings
    Was at no cost.
He admitted, right to me,
    That he would cheat,
if the situation presented itself.
I hurt inside, and cried and cried,
and needed all of my friends to help!
I feel so cheap, I feel so used,
I thought he loved me back.
I loved him with all my heart and soul!
    We had never even had a spat.
But time is lost, and so is he,
    And now my heart is broken.
I even gave back the necklace,
    Which I never took off, as a token.
A token of the love I had for him,
which now has turned to hate.
I hope what they say is true,
    "What goes around, comes around,"
    I can hardly wait!
    (4-24-1996)

Don't Go
Dedicated to Lydia Hall

I hate to see you go,
but I know you have to.
I'm devastated to see you leave,
because I know how much I'll miss you.
But when I get sad, I'll try and remember you smiling,
telling me to be happy.
I'll remember all the stories and secrets we shared.
I'll remember how much we loved each other,
and how much we cared.
I'll try and stay calm, and be prepared.
But I know that I'm losing you, and I'm really scared!
I'll write you letters, all the time.
Reminding you of the things, you had to leave behind.
But we all know that you will return to us, one day.
And when you come back, I'll make damn sure you stay!
   (2-26-1997)

Nothing

Tears roll down my cheeks; I see nothing.
My entire body shakes in pain and fear, but I feel nothing.
Anything that goes down must come back up;
I eat nothing.
I try to reach out for comfort, but I touch nothing.
The tears roll,
The shakes come,
The food comes back,
And the comfort is gone.
There is nothing. Nothing but my own despair.
The sky turns black, and the rivers dry,
as the wind blows.
The end has finally come, my end.
Soon the tears and shakes and fear will be gone.
All gone; forever.
And as death rears its ugly head in my presence,
the comfort returns.
Soon I will be at peace.
   (9-11-1996)

My Pain

Pain. What is the worst pain there is?
Cuts, scrapes, and bruises…all minor things.
The deepest pain of all is inside.
When you are all alone inside yourself,
and feel like you could never break free.
This is the pain that I feel.
This is my pain.
When everyone tells you everything is your fault,
even though you know that's not true.
Only friends can comfort you,
but they've been taken away.
Everything in your world has been taken away,
including your will to live.
The only sanctuary you have is yourself.
You are all alone!
Alone…while everything in your world seems to slip through your fingers.
You feel as though the only way to escape is to curl up into a ball and disappear.
When you hit this point, you hit the bottom.
As I have now done, and done before.
My hope for others is that they can move on.
My only hope for me, is that the next time I hit the bottom,
I am obliterated into nothing but a puddle of blood.
   (9-11-1996)

Deep Inside

There is this thing inside me that moves and breaths.
I don't know why it comes to me now.
This tiny, little thing has become a huge problem
in my life.
I don't know what to do.
I feel it growing deep inside, but I don't want it to.
Now is not the time.
I want this thing, but not today.
Years from now is when it should grow.
I love you little one, you know we both do.
But now cannot become the time for me to have you.
   (2-3-1997)

Tears

Tears of pain are not one of the things
lucky enough to be unknown by me.
Tear of pain drip from my cheeks,
though I so unwillingly set them free.
Tears and sobs and cries for what I want,
never seem to matter.
Each and every single formed drop hits my flesh
with one precise little splatter.
Never again will this flowage stop from its source.
Never did I believe the man I strived for
would let me down, with so little remorse.
I somehow always pictured us together in my mind.
But somehow fate has left me just one step behind.
   (8-9-1997)

Invisible

Looking inside of her sweet, tender eyes
you can see she's trying to hide herself from the world.
But if you look deep, the glossy protective layer vanishes
and reveals a horrible secret.
She has become a victim, a victim of a horrible disease
that she once controlled, but that now controls her.
She seems to get thinner, and thinner, and thinner.
What could possibly be so wrong?
This disease, this monster has told her that
She is ugly,
she is worthless,
she is fat.
But she is the most precious, most fragile, most beautiful
little thing you have ever seen.
She can no longer handle the sight of food,
she doesn't want to, but she forces herself to eat
so no one will know.
Then in the privacy of a quiet bathroom,
the food is flushed away,
not ever even having the chance to be digested.
She is weakening with each passing day.
Very soon, slowly but surely she will wither away.
   (10-21-1997)

Empty

Why once again have I come to this place?
A place where sorrow and despair reign.
A place where suicide is erotic and inviting.
Why, my sweetest, have you chosen
to ignore my pitiful life?
Why must you give me mixed signals of love and war?
I do not understand how one person
can cause such hatred.
Now my friend has turned to the wind and will no longer
speak in words to me.
Fleeing away the others follow in silence
and leave me an empty world.
Emptiness is a funny thing, when it fills everything
you've ever known.
   (2-16-1998)

Deep Breath

Coldness and pain.
Like a thousand and one pins stabbing you.
They poke in sharply and pull back the life
That you once breathed.
No longer is breath available for your lungs to live.
No longer is life available for those like yourself.
Sink to the watery grave that you have built up forever in your mind.
   (2-16-1998)

Cryptics

Keep watch on your life and what you do
in it.
Life is a gift to yourself, so don't abuse what
life you have left.
Memories will reign forever in the heart, though
eventually you may forget them.
Never let go of the hopes you have. They
open your eyes to the
world around you.
   (2-16-1998)

Blink

Grip the rail
hold it tight
don't let go
unless you're ready for flight.
Far below
lies the sea
and you know within it
lies your destiny.
   (2-16-1998)

Perfect Image

You look and see the image.
The image of that person.
The one you know the name, and hate just the same!
Rumor has this once set as a bitch, or so they say.
She speaks her mind and will not be told otherwise.
She does not know what she wants for life,
though she strives to achieve it.
You do not know her, you do not know the person.
You know the rumor of her demandingness.
She is not like you.
She is not like your friends.
She is herself. The person no one understands.
The one on the outside is not the one who lives.
The one you see and hear of is not who she is.
She is herself, her own, and no one knows.
   (3-17-1998)

Tear Drops

Tear drops fall
Smiles fade
Feelings die
So do I.
   (7-10-1998)

Endings

I suddenly feel like an insignificant nothing.
Why am I the last to be thought of when
the world is ending?
Why is it my fault that nothing works out alright?
Why do I not take a knife to my wrist,
or a gun to my head?
Just an end to my life.
It drags…drags on into the depths of the pits of hell,
where I have lived these past years.
And will live when I take my life away from here.
   (7-10-1998)

An Absolute Queasiness

The knots in my stomach
are giving me the feeling
of an absolute queasiness;
Thanks to him.
His smiling face
plagues my mind
more than the pains
in my stomach make
my food come back up.
I want to cry because
I feel more than alone in my life.
I only wish I could know
what it would be like
to be held by this gorgeous creature.
I want to die, I'm so alone right now.
If only he could visit me in the still of the night.
Kiss my cheek with his soft lips
and tell me honestly that I was beautiful in his eyes.
I would be content to lay next to him
in my motionless bed
'till the day I lay motionless in my eternal grave.
   (7-10-1998)

Who is That?

A teardrop falls and splashes lightly on her pale skin,
but no one notices, for she quickly wipes it away.
Her heart calls out for her to stop,
but no one notices because they are not listening.
She lifts her wrist in silent rage.
No one notices what is about to happen.
One swift slice releases spattering spurts.
And everyone notices the body
lying in the pool of blood.
   (2-16-1998)

The Way You Feel

It's the way you feel when you learn
your best friend has just died,
by decapitation.
It's the way you feel when you learn
your cat has climbed a tree and is stuck,
on the electric wire, fried.
It's the way you feel when you learn
your better half has third degree burns
over 99% of their body,
and has one hour to live.
It's the way you feel when you learn
your mother had a relationship with
Charles Manson,
and you may be the result.
It's the way you feel when you learn
your life really meant nothing,
and you die lonely and alone.
It's the way you feel when you learn your
entire purpose on this Earth
was to fertilize the weeds.
It's the way you feel when you learn
you actually never felt anything,
only numbness.
It's the way you feel when you feel nothing at all.
   (2-16-1998)

Violation

He speaks…
I hear the words that come from his mouth,
but I do not understand.
Why do you speak in tongues to me?
Why do you rip my soul?
Why don't you love the person I am?
And why won't you let me go?
   (2-13-2001)

Treatments Will Work

I feel it—it's still there!
Why won't they go away?
I treat and treat,
but they stay and stay.
Why won't you just go away?
I imagine the day when you're no longer there.
I can run, skip, and hop free from fear of pain.
You hold down
my feet on the ground.
You keep me always in your grasp.
But no more—no more.
I see you, but in my head you are letting go.
You are slowly dying.
I won't stop—I'm warning you.
I'll never stop until you're dead and gone.
Until your presence is but a painful memory.
You mine as well start on your way—it won't be long.
Soon you will be dead and gone—
Forever.
   (2-20-2001)

My Heart Aches

My heart aches for you every day, why can't you stay?
My head shows your face to me, so beautiful and full of glee.
My body slows and waits for you. Has yours slowed down too?
My fingers reach far and wide. Why have you chosen to hide?
It can't be me, it must be you, thinking you know what to do.
The taste of you lips and their feel, reminds me that this once was real.
We have been hurt, it is no lie. Why did you have to die?
   (1-14-2005)

Don't Forget

I will never love again.
I have come to realize.
Boys will be boys
Who only tell lies.
Why bother with them?
What's the fucking point?
I need to ease my pain
So let's go smoke a joint.
Here is the reason,
I always knew why.
I don't let them get to me
They just make me cry.
Never trust what they say
Or even how they act.
It is not how they are
As a matter of fact!
Remember this moment and
Remember this pain
Boys have nothing to offer,
I have nothing to gain.
   (1-24-2005)

Chapter 6:

My Animosity Amuses Me

The Mother Fucker

Mother fucker, cock sucker
Piece of shit, without wit
No one there, have no care
Tantrum time, have a fit.

Breaking glass, stupid ass
Dropping tears, full of fears
All alone, never home
Find a way, dream today.

Waste of time, never mine
Fooling me, serenity
Canceled plans, on the lam
Minutes three, unlike me.

Softer still, take a pill
Make it right, sex tonight
More than 3, that is me
Good sex too, but not with you.
   (1-12-2005)

Walk Free

I feel it—a new beginning.
One without disease and disgust.
One where I can walk barefoot
across the floor without worry.
One where I can play in the sand all day
or lay on the beach all night.
One where you are nowhere in sight
And one where you will never be seen again.
One where life is happy and bodies are free…
Free to walk the sands of all the oceans of the world.
Free to walk the sidewalks of the city
and the hallways of the schools.
Free from this disease and all others alike.
Where this begins—you end.
And that time is now.
   (2-20-2001)

Crazy Dead Boy

I have so much crazy right now.
I wish I knew when and why and how.
Insanity is coming to my head.
Stupid asshole, you're so dead.
I will make you hurt and make you pay.
Only children act this way.
You have no remorse for leading me on.
Missing you'll be, dead and gone.
I warned you not to take this path.
I warned you of such revenge and wrath.
I told you one thing, just don't lie.
You're now in grave danger, so say goodbye!
   (1-24-2005)

Cheater

Away I walk, for I am no more.
My love has gone from this river, to the shore.
He has betrayed my trust, and broken my heart.
I never thought that on that day, we would part.
He is a liar, and a potential cheater.
He told me he would cheat, if he ever did meet her.
A girl, in which, her body was better, and more divine.
I feel so cheap, and so very used that he would ever trade someone else's for mine.
I thought he loved me, and I thought he cared.
He had vowed always to protect me,
and to always be there.
But his vows, I learned, were so very thin.
It pains me to know that he does not realize,
   or even care, how much I hurt deep within.
   (4-29-1996)

Shame on Him

Fuck him, feelings dim
Retched rat, heart attack
Coma now, die somehow
Feel it here, have no fear.

Time is done, have no one
Flee this place, without haste
Run away, do not play
No more games, only shame.
   (1-12-2005)

Rape

I know you'll take me, so have some sympathy.
You'll make some heat, for you it's bitter sweet.
You'll have a day, having fun your way.
As you torture me, I'm no longer free.
As you hold me down, on the dark, cold ground.
You push inside, and I try to hide.
You grab and pinch, and I try to flinch,
You touch and feel, this can't be real!
Far below, lies all you know.
And as I thrive in pain, you do what you wanted, and came.
I lay and bleed, as you finish your dirty deed.
   (4-21-1997)

Wasting Time

Just look at me.
Here I stand again,
not knowing how,
not knowing when.
I am such a fool,
no brains in my head.
I'm starting to think,
I wish I were dead.
It just seems easier,
than dealing with pain.
What does life offer?
I have nothing to gain.
Every chance that I take,
reminds me again why,
I do not let myself,
Care about a guy.
I opened my heart
and tried for true love.
I am obviously cursed
from high above.
Do not let yourself
care more for this boy,
he is not the one,
he is just a toy.
I want to strangle him,
until his face turns blue.
Why do you do this?
What's wrong with you?
You don't even know me,
how could you care?

You always cancel our plans,
you're never even there.
Just let him go,
return to your place.
All this time spent,
nothing but a waste.
   (1-11-2005)

To Death

Are you vulnerable?
You bet you are!
Did you know that you are dying?
Right now—I see you dying.
Go ahead—try and hide.
I can find you.
I will find you!
No matter what it takes to be rid of you.
You will wither more every day.
Your life is ending.
You're dying—right now, right here.
You're on the way—on your way to hell,
Where all little diseases like you end up.
You will leave this world in pain
only to be in a million times as much pain.
Soon—very soon.
You are vulnerable to my ways,
my thoughts, my strength.
I'm stronger than you.
And soon—you will lose this battle.
   (2-20-2001)

Cease

Away with you, with your ways, your kind.
Enough is enough and this pain is time to end.
You will leave me now…far, far away.
Wherever you go—I couldn't care less.
As long as it's not here—
not here, not anywhere in my life.
The time has come for your disease to cease!
   (2-20-2001)

Revenge

Wishing you were here,
to lie in my bed.
It's now my turn
to fuck with your head.
Telling you things
you long to hear.
Holding you close
and pulling you near.
But then I'll rise,
and leave you there.
Alone in the dark,
with no underwear.
Letting you wonder,
on your way.
I don't want you here,
you cannot stay.
You broke my heart,
again and again.
Now you will question,
where and when.
Payback's a bitch,
wouldn't you say?
Out the door with you,
be on your way.
I can't stand you here,
telling me lies.
Don't even bother,
with emotionless goodbyes.
I want you out—
out of my bed,
Out of my mind—
and out of my head!
   (8-24-2001)

Baby JD

Am I mad?
I thought things were going well.
But after last weekend,
Everything went to hell!
He seemed so sweet, ah how refreshing.
But then he changed, oh so depressing.
I should have known,
I should have seen it!
They always say it,
but never mean it.
I should know so much better by now!
It's the same old shit again.
Never let them in,
Keep your head clear and remember when;
When you said this same thing to yourself,
when it happened last time.
I'm going in circles
And losing my mind.
I cannot believe I let him get to me,
How stupid am I?
Here I go again,
Falling for another guy.
I haven't even known him
for hardly that long.
I should have first thought
and known it was wrong.
Sleep with him right away,
and find their potential.
Because for me it's true,
good sex is essential.

As any aspect of a relationship, only this is true.
I thought I had found something new.
Someone different, not the same young stud,
Learning about life, a young new bud.
He has so much to find, so much to learn.
But for him, I no longer yearn.
   (1-11-2005)

Son of a Bitch

Son of a bitch, that selfish pig
On our plans, he'll re-nig
Cancel again, tell me when
You will stay, and I'll have my way.

This isn't right, I'm full of spite
Strangled and dead, off with his head
Feelings hurt, lay in dirt
Fast away, I cannot stay.

Keep me clear, when they appear
Know the signs, learn them wise
Men don't know, I am no hoe
I seek my match, feelings attach.

This is your chance, to advance
Tell me how, you feel right now
Stay or go, just let me know
Be with me, or set me free.
   (1-12-2005)

Watch Your Back

Empty promises are all that he gave.
He should be ashamed of how he's behaved.
I should be shot for letting him in.
With the touch of his hand and his sweet-looking grin.
He had his chance to bail on us, just last week.
I should have known then, the way he kissed my cheek.
He led me on, but it's unclear why.
No matter now, he simply must die.
I warned him before, don't fuck with my head.
He said of course, but he still mislead.
He will most certainly pay, for this pain I now feel.
He lied to me and told me this was real.
Watch your back you stupid little boy.
You will be sorry, for acting so coy.
I will make you wish that we never met.
You have not seen anything yet!
   (1-24-2005)

Printed in the United States
47528LVS00002B/340-387